SMOKING LOVELY: THE REMIX

SMOKING LOVELY: THE REMIX

Willie Perdomo

Haymarket Books
Chicago, Illinois

Published in 2021 by
Haymarket Books
P.O. Box 180165
Chicago, IL 60618
773-583-7884
www.haymarketbooks.org
info@haymarketbooks.org

ISBN: 978-1-64259-463-8

Distributed to the trade in the US through Consortium Book Sales and Distribution (www.cbsd.com) and internationally through Ingram Publisher Services International (www.ingramcontent.com).

This book was published with the generous support of Lannan Foundation and Wallace Action Fund.

Special discounts are available for bulk purchases by organizations and institutions. Please call 773-583-7884 or email orders@haymarketbooks.org for more information.

Cover artwork and design by Brett Nieman.

Printed in Canada by union labor.

Library of Congress Cataloging-in-Publication data is available.

10 9 8 7 6 5 4 3 2 1

CONTENTS

INTRODUCTION:
THE EMBODIED SPACES OF *SMOKING LOVELY*

Back in 2003, I was at the book party for Willie Perdomo's *Smoking Lovely* at Bar 13 in the East Village. In that venue, which had become a hub for a younger generation of poets of color associated with the slam community, Perdomo was already an icon: author of the seminal *Where a Nickel Costs a Dime* (1996) and the standout Afro-Puerto Rican voice from the foundational Nuyorican Poets Café slam scene of the early 1990s. My overriding memory of that night is the body heat emanating from the packed house giving way to laughter, cheers, and gasps as Perdomo dove into the riotous yet heartbreaking punchlines of his sophomore collection. It was a breath of fresh air and a punch in the gut at the same time.

Reading the book over the next few weeks at home and on the subway, I was struck by its indomitable wit and its trademark tone: ironic, dark, abject, but also tricksterishly funny, soulful, fearless, and full of insurrectionary rhythms. *Smoking Lovely* was the first book of Nuyorican poetry (and indeed one of the first works of art, period) to document and critique the emergence of what anthropologist Arlene Dávila called in the subtitle to her 2004 book *Barrio Dreams*, "the neoliberal city." This was the new, post-9/11 New York City of gentrification, privatization, global capital, and the so-called War on Terror all conspiring to displace, discipline, and/or disappear its most vulnerable bodies: Black and Brown, immigrant and diasporic, poor and working-class. Along with Ernesto Quiñónez's novel *Bodega Dreams* (2000), *Smoking Lovely* is one of the foundational texts of antigentrification Nuyorican literature, inspiring a whole generation of poets in their attempts to survive and subvert the neoliberal city.

1

The imprint of *Smoking Lovely* is evident in the self-reflexive street poetics of Bonafide Rojas's *Pelo Bueno: A Day in the Life of a Nuyorican Poet* (2004); in the hip-hop-coded mythic autobiography of Lemon Andersen's *Ready Made Real* (2004), whose title is taken from *Smoking Lovely*'s "Spotlight at the Nuyorican Poets Café"; in the fusion of diasporic insurrection and dystopian irony in Not4Prophet's *Last of the Po'Ricans y Otros Afro-Artifacts* (2013); and even in the non-slammer global punchlines of my own books *Boringkén* (2008) and *Hi-Density Politics* (2010). Beyond New York, the book was crucial in shaping the self-reflexive poetics of complicity in Guillermo Rebollo Gil's *Teoría de conspiración* (2005), with its autoethnographic insights into the raced and classed geospatial construction and commodification of "poesía urbana" (urban poetry) in Puerto Rico. It is also an important point of reference for Chicano poet (and veteran of the Taco Shop Poets collective) Tomás Riley in his debut book *Mahcic* (2006), whose anti-capitalist barrio flow engages San Diego and San Francisco's Mission District in ways that echo Perdomo's Nuyorican lyric tableaux.

As I note in my critical study *In Visible Movement: Nuyorican Poetry from the Sixties to Slam* (2014), a poem like "Spotlight at the Nuyorican Poets Café" is essential in staging *Smoking Lovely*'s explorations of poetry and the neoliberal city at the intersection of community and commodity. In this radically revised new edition, Perdomo shifts the poem into mostly second person, thereby further accentuating its introspective and complex exploration of self-and/as-other, and of the simultaneous othering, commodification, and spectacularization of Afro-diasporic bodies and cultural forms:

> *Since then, you have become a street poet*
> *Somebody's favorite urban poet*
> *A new-jack hip-hop rap poet*
> *A spoken word artist*
> *A born-again Langston Hughes*
> *A downtown performance poet*
> *But you won't be caught rehearsing—*
> *your spit is ready made real*

The book's abject and irreverent body politics are framed by the title poem, which begins:

When you smoke crack
everything is measured by

how fast your face melts.

The layers of irony in the title compound, as "smoking lovely" evokes drug use but also the dystopian beauty of a post-9/11 New York in glitzy, marketable ruins, with the sociopolitical visions of earlier generations of Nuyorican poets seemingly up in smoke. The publication of *Smoking Lovely* coincided with the global hegemony of Russell Simmons's Def Poetry empire (epitomized by the HBO series *Def Poetry*) and its commodification of a brand of slam and hip-hop poetics, yet Perdomo's book calls out poetry as commodity, and is closer to the work of foundational Nuyorican poet (and rap poetry forerunner) Miguel Piñero, who cofounded the Nuyorican Poets Café with Miguel Algarín and others. Like Piñero's work, *Smoking Lovely* is a deliberately raw and loaded exploration of the devastation of Black and Brown bodies but also an attempt to reimagine urban space from the perspective of what the late Juan Flores called, in *The Diaspora Strikes Back* (2007), "diaspora from below." In his "A Lower East Side Poem" (*La Bodega Sold Dreams*, 1980), Piñero takes a perverse pride in being "a cancer of Rockefeller's ghettocide," in effect embracing his abjectly racialized and classed Nuyorican body as a space of contestation, and ultimately reimagining the Lower East Side as an untranslatable affective space (i.e., Loisaida), where new poetic and political possibilities take shape. Piñero is evoked in "Spotlight" as "Mikey the Junky Christ, creator of the Ghetto Genesis where Shit begat Fucked Up," and his outlaw, existential remapping of the city animates poems like "Franklin Avenue Snack Box," with its heartfelt evocation of a trans-Caribbean, pandiasporic Brooklyn, where "Biggie's oxtails" and "African butter soap" coexist among dollar stores and where "The only Puerto Rican/flag on the block/looks like it's crying."

As tricky as the authenticity politics of "Spotlight" might be ("ready made real" could be read as a diss of the "ready-made" realness of the neoliberal city and its pro forma slammers and MCs), the figure of Reverend Pedro Pietri is invoked at the end of the poem in a way that further aligns it with an outlaw Nuyorican tradition and outside the market pragmatism of the neoliberal city. As our new jack street poet gets onstage at the Nuyorican Poets Café, "the good Reverend Pedro hands you a condom and says, 'Here, man. You never know what you might catch up there.'" Pietri was of course famous for handing out poems as part of his brilliantly anarchic performances, partly in keeping with his AIDS activism but also aligned with his antifoundationalist and anticolonial poetics, which stressed a ritual confrontation with death in life (as in his "Rent-a-Coffin" performances and his classic book *Puerto Rican Obituary*) as an essential part of personal and poetic liberation. While there is a doubtless homosocial heteromasculinism in this scene, there is also great power in how Perdomo reclaims an often-pathologized Nuyorican/Afro-Latino masculinity through the imperatives of solidarity and self-care.

By aligning his book with a Nuyorican tradition of innovative poetics of resistance, Perdomo is also positioning *Smoking Lovely* as a departure from his debut *Where a Nickel Costs a Dime*, a book whose difficult yet luminous Harlem autoethnographies still fit within the parameters of the multicultural literary landscape that was emerging in the 1990s. If that first book spoke from Harlem to the world, *Smoking Lovely* by contrast doubled down on the particular, the messy, the culturally specific, the untranslatable. This was an exceedingly gutsy thing to do from a career perspective, as it risked alienating the wider readership that had been so welcoming of Perdomo's first book. In fact, *Smoking Lovely*, published with a spoken-word CD by the tiny imprint of the esteemed downtown literary magazine *Rattapallax*, which Perdomo helped edit for a time, was a decidedly modest commercial success. A *Publishers Weekly* review rightly praised the power of Perdomo's performances and rapid-fire enjambments, but also argued their power was often "lost in transcription." Beyond the long-standing undervaluation of performance-oriented poetries, what is most surprising about that review is that it missed what is perhaps the most noteworthy aspect of *Smoking Lovely*'s poetics on the page: its eccentric experiments with the prose poem.

"Ten-Pound Draw" is emblematic of Perdomo's prose-poetic method. Freed from the expectation of delivering lyric epiphanies, the poet spreads out, exploring the inner and outer geographies of belonging and exclusion. The Spanglish here emerges as a radically translingual vernacular, closer to dub poetry, which is fitting given its Black and Brown UK setting. When Black girls racialize the poem's speaker as Pakistani, the speaker acidly replies, "I say that I am Nuyorikistani, so I talk como like this y como like that y como like kikireeboo mandinga, *no doubt, it's all good, I am all of that if you want me to be.*" Afro-Latinx invisibility (or blurred visibility) is further coded here through the reference to the classic "kikiribu mandinga" refrain from Guillermo Rodríguez Fiffe's iconic Afro-Cuban guaracha "Bilongo" (aka "La Negra Tomasa"). The misreading of an Afro-Latino as Pakistani (a doubly loaded scene in post-9/11 London) also brings to mind the generic use of the term "Mandingo" in the West, to a range of African peoples. Of course, the speaker's *"no doubt, it's all good, I am all of that if you want me to be"* performs and parodies the scripts of Blackness in the context of Empire as it structures the poem. The loose narrative structure evokes a range of narrative forms (manifesto, journal, etc.), while the clause-heavy sentences give the poem a breathless, improvisational quality that echoes its investment in Black expressive cultures.

If there is a precedent for the pandiasporic prose experiments in *Smoking Lovely*, it is surely Jean Toomer's modernist classic *Cane* (1923). While *Cane* is typically thought of as a novel, its open-ended and nonlinear structure of poetic vignettes complicates genre conventions while evoking the fractal geographies of diaspora. In claiming both the Harlem Renaissance and the Nuyorican tradition, Perdomo paves the way for a younger generation of Afro-Latinx poets whose work challenges the ethnic and racial silos that still dominate US publishing and academia. Of course, not every experiment in *Smoking Lovely* is successful, which is likely why Perdomo has produced the condensed and revised edition you have in your hands. The revisions largely heighten the tension and impact of the book's experiments, and to my mind all the crucial poems from the original edition are included here.

When I asked Perdomo if I could interview him for my 2014 book, *In Visible Movement: Nuyorican Poetry from the Sixties to Slam*, he politely and graciously declined. It's not hard to see why. Evidently, Perdomo was unhappy with some of the poems, and the book documented a personal and political moment that the author presumably did not want to dwell on so many years later. More simply, Perdomo's poetry had changed, and New York City and the world had, too. His next book of poetry, *The Essential Hits of Shorty Bon Bon* (2014), was a book of openings, new beginnings, and rediscoveries (family history, Puerto Rico, a hidden salsa of the 1970s in the shadow of Fania), published late in the Obama age, in the context of increased institutional visibility for Black writers in the US. By contrast, in *Smoking Lovely* we feel the world closing in, the death rattle of 1990s multiculturalism and globalization fantasies. I am glad it is back in print, so we can learn from it in these dark times. As opposed to the essentialized barrio of Latinx literary stereotypes, Perdomo investigates the production of urban space by corporations and the state and also by our acts of resistance and imagination. Its politics are structural. It affords us a new way to read the city—not just New York City, but all our neglected cities, as we figure out a way between the bodies of our dead and the spectralities of our debt, between the respective ghosts and dreams of our colonial histories, between "writing poetry/in the middle of marketing meetings/looking for a way/to position our story" and "the hip-hop of our new sun language," with which we write "the next line of poetry by which the world/will choose to live." (From, "Electronic Kites" and "Open Mic at Make the Road by Walking, Inc.")

Perdomo's trajectory has been crucial in shaping the contours of socially engaged twenty-first-century Puerto Rican poetry. In addition to his defining work on the US mainland, he was (along with Mariposa Fernández), the first Nuyorican poet of the post-1980s generation to build and sustain relationships with young poets in Puerto Rico, thus prefiguring the increased collaboration between poets in Puerto Rico and the diaspora that has proven so decisive in our present austerity-ravaged yet activism-rich moment. Perdomo founded the #PoetsforPuertoRico readings that were so crucial in the aftermath of Hurricane Maria, and his work continues to inspire, and evolve in conversation with, that of poets from Puerto Rico as important as José Raúl "Gallego" González and Raquel Salas Rivera (not to mention myself, again). Of course, Perdomo's work as a poet and mentor has been invaluable in shaping an increasingly visible younger generation of Afro-Latinx poets, and his work has long centered the experience of Black people across the diaspora in ways that challenge US and Latin American racial logics.

Crucial in this respect is "Forty-One Bullets Off Broadway," about the 1999 shooting death of unarmed Guinean immigrant Amadou Diallo at the hands of New York police officers who shot him forty-one times outside his Bronx apartment and were later acquitted of murder. Perdomo's elegy gruesomely yet hauntingly finds in Diallo's dead body a "connect-the-dots picture of Africa," imagining a pandiasporic geography that spans El Barrio (East Harlem) and the Bronx: "From the Bronx to El Barrio, we heard you fall face first/into the lobby of your equal opportunity,/forty-one bullets like silver pushpins/holding up a connect-the-dots picture of Africa." The term "Off Broadway" ruefully marks the simultaneous spectacularization of Black death and the invisibility of the Black body. Anticipating #Black-LivesMatter, Perdomo's poem centers diaspora from below, and reminds us that true liberation (Puerto Rican and otherwise) is impossible without challenging anti-Blackness.

More than fifteen years after its initial publication, *Smoking Lovely* retains its power as a challenge to us poets and poetry-lovers to not take language as given; to read, write, and organize critically and from our own bodies; to be political not in a topical sense, but in the sense of the investigation of urban and embodied space. As Perdomo puts it at the end of the standout poem "The New Boogaloo," once again playfully invoking Pietri and Piñero, *"we gonna die knowing/how beautiful/we really are."*

This unabashedly irreverent and noncommercial book is nonetheless full of joy and humor and beauty. Its lovely depths have shaped generations of socially engaged urban poets across barrios and diasporas, modeling a personal counterhistory that confronts us with the scars we bear as empire's children while urging us forward toward radical acts of dreaming, creating, working together, and "writing our names/on the wall just to let the world know/that we were here forever."

—Urayoán Noel
The Bronx
August 2019

MAD FUNNY STYLE
A 10-Minute Play

CAST OF CHARACTERS

PABLO: *late 20s, Puerto Rican (Black, too)*

SONIA: *late 20s, Black*

WALT: *late 20s, Black*

SZU: *late 20s, Chinese American*

POET: *50s, White*

STAGE MANAGER: *20, White*

MAN: *30s, wears a pith helmet*

Where: A green room in a university theater somewhere in Amsterdam.

When: 1990s.

Who: A group of spoken-word artists at the end of a European tour.

Lights up.

Stage right is a door that leads to a bathroom. The door is closed but you can hear water running from a faucet. Stage left is the entrance to the green room. Infrequently, we hear slight static from an intercom above the entrance door. This is supposed to be a live relay of the performance but the intercom is dysfunctional. Upstage center is a full-length sofa. When the scene opens, SONIA is downstage center sitting in front of one of three dressing room mirrors that are lined with light bulbs. SONIA is in the middle of what seems to be elocution exercises when she notices a smudge in the mirror. She tries to wipe it off with a tissue. No success. She grabs a bottle of spring water, pours it on the tissue, and tries to wipe the smudge again. No success. In the bathroom you hear a finishing-up process: the rack of a towel dispenser, the drying of hands, a clearing of throat, and a toilet flushing.

PABLO *enters and watches* SONIA *rubbing the mirror voraciously.*

PABLO   You should spit on that (*throws himself on the sofa and lies down*).

SONIA   Got everybody thinking you done with that shit.

PABLO   (*ignoring her*) Walter get here yet? I left him in the red-light district last night. You would think being from New York nothing would surprise us, right? We like to think we've seen it all. We just smoked a little blueberry in a café, had some coffee, and on the way back to the hotel we stopped in front of this store. Looked like one of those fortune-teller stores. I thought I saw a woman on a swing. Maybe the blueberry had me buggin', I thought. So, we stood there for a second and there was a black velvet curtain and sure enough out of the curtain a blond woman in a red-laced bustier was sitting on a swing, swinging like she was at a playground, and right before she disappeared behind the curtain, she would open her legs, and Walt kept saying, "Look at that. Look at that. Oh shit. Look at that." If I would've died last night, the last words I would've remembered hearing were "Look at that."

PABLO *lights a cigarette.*

SONIA   (*pointing to a "no smoking" sign*) I know your mama taught you how to read.

PABLO   I missed the Dutch lesson, baby.

         (*beat*)

SONIA   Walt is one of those on-the-way brothers. Always almost getting there, but never quite getting *there there*.

PABLO   You need to stop. For real. That's what's wrong with you, you—

SONIA   Wrong is the first thing coming out of you. You ain't know right since wrong left. You need to stop.

PABLO   You need to stop working for claps. And you and I still need to talk.

SONIA   Ain't nothing to talk about. Just go shit somewhere else. Don't take us with you. This ain't the States, and a check comes with those claps if you didn't know.

         WALT *walks in laughing.* SONIA *resumes wiping the mirror.*

WALT   Yo, I just saw the illest shit. The Antillean dude we were hanging out with last night? The poet? He gets up to spit, and a stanza into his poem five white boys, calling themselves the Real Line, stand up and start reading their own work. Shit was kind of dope, like they had a mad funny style.

PABLO   And you look like you soaked in mad red light.

WALT   Now I know why.

         STAGE MANAGER *enters.*

STAGE
MANAGER   Sonia? Five minutes and you go. Yes?

SONIA   I don't do first, love.

ST. MGR.   No, second, after opening.

WALT   (*to* SONIA) I know you ain't scared of the Real Line, Sonia. They
           just part of the performance.

SONIA   (*to* ST. MGR., *reading her*) Opening of show is opening of show,
           and because we are the featured show and there's a lineup and my
           name is first on your list then I'm first. And, I repeat: I don't do first.

           ST. MGR. *speaks into her headphones.*

WALT   (*to* ST. MGR.) Our first poet is having technical difficulties with
           her mirror. It's okay. I'm first, love. I'm your first love. First. That's
           me.

           SZU *enters with* POET.

WALT   Szu, we have a problem.

SZU   They spelled my fucking name wrong on the poster is the prob-
           lem! (*to* ST. MGR.) Are you with the school? (SZU *snatches the
           headphone off of* ST. MGR.'s *head and yells into it*) Hello? Hello?
           My name is spelled S-z-u. Not S-u-e. (*shoves headphones back to*
           ST. MGR.)

ST. MGR.   I do not design the poster. (*beat*) *Kankerlijer.*

SONIA   What?

WALT   Okay, okay, touché touché. (*to* ST. MGR.) Two minutes?

ST. MGR.   Five minutes.

           ST. MGR. *exits.*

WALT   Sonia can't see herself, Szu.

SONIA   (*to* WALT *as if at the start of a game she doesn't want to play*) Stop.

SZU   She looks fine to me.

WALT   No, the mirror. There's a stain on it.

SZU   Might be old lipstick. You know, lipstick and mirrors. Spit works.

SONIA   (*pointing to* POET) Who is this?

SZU   This is my poet. Trying something new tonight. I write. He recites. Need two mics tonight. (*to* POET, *she starts*) Let me count—

POET   The days—

SONIA   Hold up.

WALT   Ohhhhhhh . . . ohhhhh . . . ohhhh, yesss, Szu. That's word.

     SONIA *moves over to* PABLO *who seems to be dreaming.* SONIA *taps his leg. No response.*

SZU   He's going to burn himself.

     SONIA *taps* PABLO *again.*

WALT   Paloma!

     PABLO *wakes.*

PABLO   Bendicion.

WALT   Let's go, dream keeper. Ready?

SONIA   No. Not tonight.

     The What Game is a sort of hype ritual before they get on stage. Sort of a Bundini/Ali thing.

WALT   What.

PABLO   A fire.

WALT   A fire on a mountain. A fire in the street. A fire in the mirror. A Black fire.

PABLO   What it do?

WALT   Riots.

PABLO   What it be?

WALT   Fuego.

PABLO   How to get there?

WALT   From the window to the wall, from the ceiling to the floor.

PABLO   If you can't hit 'em hard . . .

WALT   Kill 'em softly.

         WALT *and* PABLO *dap.* ST. MGR. *enters.*

ST. MGR.   Excuse me. Man in lobby looking for Pablo.

SONIA   He's on the way.

WALT   (*to* ST. MGR.) One man? Two man? Three?

ST. MGR.   They just say Pablo.

SZU   (*to* POET) Pablo is hot tonight. Let's go, Poet. First line out the door.

         SZU *exits with* POET.

SONIA   (*to* ST. MGR.) Pablo is not here. He's *kankerlijer.*

         ST. MGR. *exits.*

WALT   (*to* PABLO) My man, you hot tonight.

SONIA   (*to* PABLO) I can see your future and it don't come with car service.

PABLO   I'm sure there's a train running. There's always a train running. (*beat*)

A knock on the door. PABLO *walks into the bathroom and closes the door.* SONIA *opens the door and a silhouette of a man in a pith helmet appears.*

MAN   Pablo.

SONIA   Who?

MAN   Pablo. The Poet.

SONIA   He went to get me a drink, sweetheart. C'mon, let's see if we can find him.

SONIA *exits with* MAN. PABLO *comes out of the bathroom and lies back on the sofa.*

PABLO   That was the trading company wasn't it?

WALT   Some dude wearing a pith helmet. (*beat*) What you into man? Thought you was done with all that.

PABLO   Bro, I got up feeling good this morning. End of tour, last gig, back home tomorrow, getting paid, and I see Sonia sitting by herself in the hotel dining room and she looks like she been crying all night. I ask her what's wrong and I keep asking her and she says nothing, and I look at her and suddenly I remember Paloma. She cried all night, too. So, you know, I hit rewind and went there. I ask Sonia, You seeding? She says, I'm rooting. And then she says it's ours.

WALT   What?

PABLO   Yeah.

WALT   Wait. Hold up. What?

PABLO   Yeah, man.

WALT   Nah. (*points at the mirror*) Sonia?

PABLO   Sonia, bro.

WALT   Wait, que? Nah.

PABLO   That second day we had off in Paris. Shit jumped off at breakfast too, except this time there were no tears. She said she wanted to go see the *Mona Lisa*, so we went to the Louvre, did some tourist shit, looked for Black people, then walked and walked and walked and talked and talked, had some dinner and walked and walked and walked, then we went to this cool joint called Barrio Latino and danced like we were uptown. Got back to the hotel and the concierge sent us a bottle of champagne and kept singing *l'amour l'amour l'amour*. I say, cool, you know, I got no intentions. She's people. She's my sister. She says we need to finish the champagne before it gets warm. Next thing you know it's morning, and I'm making music out of the garbage truck beep, and Sonia and I are having croissants and coffee in bed and laughing.

WALT   I thought she hated you.

PABLO   Stop fucking with me, man. C'mon.

WALT   That ain't no reason to cop a taste, man.

PABLO   All day, after Sonia told me, I been thinking about Paloma. I call out for her in my sleep. No answer. I walk into the bathroom and I see her, eyes fluttering and there's blood running down her leg. Baby! Baby! I yell. It's the same all the time. I run cold water on her, fix her hair, and by the time the ambulance comes she's already turning cold and then suddenly I'm on this sofa thinking about what I wanna name the baby.

WALT   You about to go through something worse fucking with that dragon again.

PABLO   It was just one, Walt.

        (*beat*)

WALT   (*as if he's heard it before*) Time to go spit, Pablo the Poet.

        WALT *and* PABLO *dap.*

PABLO   Go get her, bro. Tell dude I left for New York last night.

        ST. MGR. *knocks.* PABLO *skirts into the bathroom.*

WALT   Hallo.

        ST. MGR. *enters.*

ST. MGR.   Walter.

WALT   Walter is ready. What is your name?

ST. MGR.   Gogh. Like painter.

WALT   You ready to go, Gogh?

ST. MGR.   Bedankt.

WALT   (*to* ST. MGR.) One minute?

ST. MGR.   So nice. One minute. Yes.

        ST. MGR. *exits.* PABLO *comes out of the bathroom.*

WALT   Time to spit, rookie. Don't forget: The van leaves from the hotel at 0600 hours tomorrow.

PABLO   You gonna be on it?

WALT   I don't think so. I think I'm gonna check out some of those Van
          Goghs.

PABLO   Walt, I'm gonna call the baby Knight.

WALT   Night? Might as well call it Day Day.

PABLO   No, man. Knight. Like Etheridge. Like armor. Like shining.

WALT   Might not be a poet.

PABLO   (*starting The What Game*) Might be.

WALT   Might not know until later.

PABLO   Might never know.

WALT   Then what?

          They dap. WALT *exits.* PABLO *goes into the bathroom humming A
          Tribe Called Quest's "I Lost My Wallet in El Segundo."* SONIA *enters
          and takes her seat at the dressing-room table. She spits on the mirror
          and wipes it clean. She is satisfied and resumes her elocution exercises.*

          The water faucet in the bathroom turns on.

          (*beat*)

          Water runs for ten long seconds.

          Lights out.

SMOKING LOVELY: THE REMIX

For my Day Ones
For the Nuyorican Poets Café
For Ed Randolph

Rest in Poetry, Carmen Perdomo, te quiero mucho madre mía
Rest in Poetry, William Perdomo, te quiero mucho padre mío

I wanna rock right now.

—Rob Base

I.   PAPO'S ARS POETICA

SPOTLIGHT AT THE NUYORICAN POETS CAFÉ

Finally fixed you get to the café in the time for your spotlight. You ask Julio the Bouncer to stay inside so he can hear you read tonight. He says only if you read something happy, none of that dark ghetto shit because tonight's crowd has already pissed him off. Julio is the best random judge in the house. "C'mon, you know you can't take this shit too seriously," he says. He strengthens your aesthetic as you walk through the door and spot the spoken-word racketeers who get close enough to dig into your pockets when you fall asleep. You just spent your last ten dollars, and they look at you stupid when you ask if they can spare some real change. You were just a poet wanting to read a poem the first night you came here.

Since then, you have become a street poet
Somebody's favorite urban poet
A new-jack hip-hop rap poet
A spoken word artist
A born-again Langston Hughes
A downtown performance poet
But you won't be caught rehearsing—
Your spit is ready made real

You walk up to the cherubic man whose smile will not close, who will allow himself to die only when love fails to create. He starts another story about his soul brother, Mikey the Junky Christ, creator of the Ghetto Genesis where Shit begat Fucked Up. Saint Miguelito who is said to have seen God and said, "Vaya, I heard you got the good shit." The cherubic man with white hair stays alive by sniffing Mikey's ashes in the Avenue D air.

You pull up to the back of the bar and sit next to the blind man who's waiting for someone to light his cigarette. "Where the hell you been?" he says. "I'm glad you're here because these motherfuckers want to cop pleas and sell Cliff's notes before they read a goddamn thing."

A guest poet from the Academy is invited to the stage. He begs the audience to be gentle because his work is really made for the page. The blind man shouts, "Shut up and read the goddamn poem."

You kiss the lady with the sunglasses that are sometimes used to deflect rays, always to look where you can't see. She's been taking notes on the scene, watching poets exchange business cards as they tap dance toward the stage. She hugs you tight and begs you to take care of yourself because the bigger picture might need you.

The impresario leaps onto the stage, grabs the mic, and tells the DJ to give him a hippity hip & a hippity hop, "Is Word Perfect in the house?"

The flame on a white prayer candle above the bar is doing the Cucaracha.

In the photo behind it, Mikey is looking dead into the camera.

Before you reach the mic, the good Reverend Pedro hands you a condom and says, "Here, man. You never know what you might catch up there."

THE DAY HECTOR LAVOE DIED

The baritone Univision broadcast thunders from the living room TV. "En las noticias hoy, El Cantante de los Cantantes, Hector Lavoe, se murio en—"

Mami Cuca yells from her dent in the sofa where the world is a telenovela, where she books flights to Miami and Mexico, and talks back to commercials.

You rub the funk out of your eyes and swallow the drip of diesel nesting at the back of your throat. You walk toward the TV glare in the living room.

"Mira lo. Se murió. Dead. Look at him. He was the best of the best, and look how he wasted away." She starts the story about the day Hector came to pick up uncle Lolé and she had to throw them out of the house for starting a mainline bang-bang in the bathroom.

You sink into the love seat and join the coro during the technicolor retrospective of a young Fania All-Star. He smiles through hazel-tinted eyeglasses. He's dressed in a pearl-white three-piece suit, silk shirt, and a giant red bow tie. We stand in the stadium, singing and clapping to his comedia tragic. The broadcast cuts to a hospitalized salsero, twisted under sterile white sheets, sunglasses too big for his face, and he waves at us with the little strength he has left.

"Coño, que flaco . . . " you say.

"Like you," Mami Cuca says. "You know why he's like that right? You know, right? She mimes an injection into the crook of her elbow.

After the tribute, you go back to your room and snort your breakfast bag knowing that you'll have to start the next day on empty. You turn off the lights, lie on the floor, stare at the ceiling, and Hector sings to you until your eyes figure skate shut. "Que problema, caballero/en que me encuentro yo." Mami Cuca continues her commentary on the breaking news. "Just like you.

He didn't have a monkey on his back. He had King Kong, baby."

Your nod invites you to a parade. Your breath is getting further away from one more chance and your face was just hyperspaced into a black sky, looking like King Tut with a shape up. This is the face-to-face appointment with the Department of Human Resources that you can't miss even if you tried. You hear a blast of trumpets, a wave of trombones, and you feel like changing directions. You follow the sun as it funnels its way through your body. The viejos stop slapping their dominoes, radios go blank, bochinche vines go dry, and you finally get to see your uncle play. He sits on a park bench with a conga between his legs. The woman next to him does not realize her hips are moving until she lets out a loud moan, begging for more. You ask him if you can collaborate as you do backstrokes in the drip at the bottom of your throat. A cigarette ash falls and taps the linoleum. Mami Cuca is talking to herself about salsa and love. Her slippers drag to the bathroom. The water pills are working extra hard today. She hums a Tito Rodriguez riff and bangs on your door, making sure you're not drowning in your vomit. You clear your throat and sigh because she fucked up your high with that same story about all that could've been in a world where the only thing left to remember is a woman putting on her nightgown, swearing to God that the night Hector Lavoe sang "El Todopoderoso" at the annual St. Paul's Mother's Day dance, the saints came down from their stained-glassed windows and started dancing.

PAPO'S ARS POETICA

I'm stuck in a poem
that looks like a mother who just lost
her only son to the last bullet of the night

Her long cries sneak under my door
like the beginning of dinner

My eyes are buried inside this poem's
avenue like peeping-tom traffic
lights checking out last night's
rite of passage, painting a dog
chasing a cat with a jungle-
boogie beatdown for his ass

My teeth bite on this poem
like the slow wind that chews
on tomorrow's myths, that brothers
be busy making on noontime
corners where my ears are stashed
on the down low

I'm stuck in this poem
like a squealing rat
caught in a discount glue trap
soaking in a fresh puddle
of piss psst pssssst—mira mami

I'm home

in the street of this poem
where I'm stuck

YOU PAY FOR WHAT YOU GET,
BUT YOU NEVER GET WHAT YOU PAY FOR

Brooklyn bound and I left my heart uptown with a Mexican mango sculptor. I should have known something was wrong when Satan stopped singing the blues in front of the Studio Museum. Last night, the Queen of Sugar Hill slipped into a new storefront and ran off with the councilman who was up all night keeping his eyes on the prize. Street corners were taken over by corn-row hustlers and Kente-cloth syndicates. Coffee chains, T-shirt clubs, and ringing Taco Bells got the magazines saying that our communities are safe and clean, but the other day I kissed a girl who had a monster in her blood and didn't even know it. Wrecking balls are aimed at the heads of housing projects. The world is getting baggy with brand names and producers are taking hip-hop seminars so they can keep it real. There's an invisible billboard on the side of the state office building. It's a promotion for the platinum-selling single, "You Don't Have to Go Home, But You Gots to Get the Fuck Out of Here." This morning, buses disguised as historic neighborhood tours came and stole all the queen's brownstones. Homeless Man went checking for leftovers. He walked by a silver-studded prophet who was preaching in front of a subway station, waving a star that had six points, and Homeless Man said, "Sheeeeeet, even if God did have an Afro, I still ain't got nowhere to live."

NEW JACK CITY

Ain't nothing new about
new jack hustlers

They might be using
computers to count

but they still hire
guns for insurance

FRANKLIN AVENUE SNACK BOX

London fogs
Eastern Parkway

Benches are drenched
in colonial dew

You stop at the 99 CENTS
store for some Mistolín &

Get something and
wave everybody and

Everything costs more
than a dollar

Get something and wave

You cop a ganja sack before
beat cops turn the corner

Big Black talking
penal jazz

Took a flat five
last time he was
in Sing Sing

The only Puerto Rican
flag on the block
looks like it's crying

Biggie's oxtails &
British Empire heels
stomp on the downtown
2 Train

Angry nurses
curse sick-passenger delays
and whoever gave birth
to *that Bomboclaat boy*

Hasidim stride by
African butter soap

Crusty crackheads
race pit bulls

Hairdressers take tonic
juice breaks

You cradle your single-man dinner:
a thigh, a leg, and a bun

Waiting for the green light
a schoolgirl reads a gangster
who calls her his sun

SHOULD OLD SHIT BE FORGOT

Papo the Poet started kicking a poem
while Dick Clark put the city on the count:

Once again, we pledge
down for whatever
until the day we die

Love forever in one
minute it takes sixty
seconds to forget the
one who left you

And Brother Lo was like:

"All that shit you sayin'
sounds good but let's talk
about the $30 you owe me

I hear you I hear you I hear
what you're saying—
we boys and we should be
happy when big-ass disco
balls drop on 151-proof
resolutions

Father Time says
he's only gonna smoke
on the weekends

New Year cornets
are swept off the street
like old friends

Champagne corks ricochet
off ballroom walls

Roast pork burns while we
puff & pass in project halls

Bullets kill El Barrio sky and
the same ole same ole shit
we say every year

Fuck it
pass that rum
it's cold out here—
who wants some?

You could say *please*
You could freeze
Whatever is clever

Happy New Years
Felíz Año Nuevo

I'm out here for a reason
not the season
should old shit be forgot
and all that good stuff

But I want my money
before next year."

BROTHER LO AND THE MAXIMS

NYPD siren light splashed across Brother Lo's storm-colored eyes. He assumed his science-dropping stance. He lit a cigarette, puffed hard, and exhaled a jet stream of menthol into the wind. Then he said:

"Man in East Harlem lives according to a set of maxims. *What comes around goes around.* That's a maxim. Like a merry-go-round. But more like you chillin' on your stoop one day, sipping on the dregs of a Mister Softee vanilla shake, you turn your head, and a face you thought you forgot smiles at you and sticks a Rambo knife into your heart. That's for that shit you did when you was a kid, he says. What went around came around.

"Payback is a bitch, but revenge is a motherfucker. Like maxim number one. Except the mysterious mug wipes the blade clean with your hair, spits on you, kicks you in the jaw, and laughs like the villain in your favorite gangster movie.

"Bullets ain't got no names. Lately, you been trying to live on the good side of the street. You get off a train stop before yours, decline party invitations, and walk around the block instead of down the avenue. One night you decide to go to sleep early. You just finished writing a long love letter to your ex, and your mother's boyfriend smoked your bedtime Newport. You go to Gadda-fi's twenty-four-hour counter. You see Charlie Rock. He's running the block now. He asks you where you been because he ain't been seeing you around. *Just chillin',* you say when the clapping starts, shells clink, your skin tingles like the needles you swore never to use, and beyond the rainbow oil puddle where you lie, somebody yells for your mother who just heard you whisper *goodbye* from the ceiling. You told your ex that you wanted death to be sure when it pulled up, and instead you got hit by a bullet with no name."

FORTY-ONE BULLETS OFF BROADWAY

For Amadou Diallo

It's not like you were looking at a vase
filled with plastic white roses
while pissing in your mother's toilet
and hoped that today was not the day
you bumped into four cops
who happened to wake up
with a bad case of contagious shooting.

From the Bronx to El Barrio
we heard you fall face first
into the lobby of your equal opportunity,
forty-one bullets like silver pushpins
holding up a connect-the-dots picture of Africa.

Forty-one bullets
not giving you enough time
to hit the floor
with dignity and justice for all,
forty-one bullet shells
trickling onto the bubble-gum-stained mosaic
where your body was mapped out.

Before your mother kissed you goodbye,
she forgot to tell you that American kids
get massacred in daycare,
slaughtered during Sunday sermons;
they are mourned for a whole year
while people like you go away quietly.

Before you could show your ID and say, *Officer*—
four regulation glock clips went achoo
and smoked you into spirit,
and by the time a special street unit

decided what was enough,
another dream submitted an application for deferral.

It was *la vida te da sorpresas,*
sorpresas te da la vida/ay Dios
and you probably thought I was singing
"La Vida Loca" but be you prince,
be you pauper, the skin on your drum
makes you the usual suspect around here.

By the time you hit the floor
protest poets came to your rescue,
legal eagles opened extra phone lines,
booked red-eyes to New York, and stuffed
file folders with dream-team pitches for
your mother who side-eyed your defense,
because Justice has been known to keep one
eye open for the right price.

By the time you hit the floor,
the special unit forgot everything they learned
at the Academy.
The mayor told them to take paid leave,
and when they returned, he sent them to go
beat up a million young Black men
while your blood seeped
through the tiles in the lobby
of your equal opportunity—
from the Bronx to El Barrio
there were enough shots
to go around.

THE FLOOD

When God sent
the Flood,
his mama said:

*Mop that mess off
the floor, boy.*

And God said:

*That ain't mess, Mami.
Those are tears.
Some for sorrow,
some for joy.*

II.   STOP SIGNS

TENDERLOIN

The guy in the tweed blazer said he came west to chill.

Johnny Shakespeare from Harlem.

Every two days he checked in to shoot tar and watch
snow on a secondhand TV.

They can wait, he said.

He checked for his wallet as he watched an Aztec chief spray-
paint a self-portrait on a brick wall.

"Love could still work when I get back home," he said.

On the BART back to Oakland he went through his
file of excuses:

The police put him jail for talking to the ghost of Huey
Newton on the top step of the Alameda County Courthouse.

He was trying to restore the face of the Virgin de Guadalupe.

He was kidnapped by a department store security squad
who thought that he was a member of Al-Qaeda.

He was robbed and had to perform poetry for train fare.

He met two girls who had a tweed blazer fetish.

He went to Fisherman's Wharf and recreated a romantic
weekend he once had with Laura.

He needed to get his thoughts together, so he walked up &
down the Crookedest Street in the World.

He turned into a penthouse panther and went prowling through the streets, looking for someone to finance the revolution.

SMOKING LOVELY

When you smoke crack
everything is measured by

how fast your face melts.

If I can pull your eyes
out of their sockets and

your cheekbones bruise
me when I hug you or

your lips scratch mine
when we kiss, then you

must be smoking lovely.

OH SHIT, BLUES

I got a feeling my woman is playing me dirty
Said I got a feeling my woman is playing me dirty
Her declarations of love been awfully wordy

SEESAW LOVE SONG

Spent a whole day and night
playing on my seesaw

See if I could forget
Saw that it was over
before it started

I never change
the way I get over it

I go up in smoke and
come down in a nod
I go up in smoke and
come down in a nod

Then I promise to stop
as soon as I finish the last one

So I go up in smoke,
come down in a nod
I go up in smoke,
come down in a nod

And tell myself
that everything is alright
I can live without her
as long as I have
my seesaw

ELECTRONIC KITES

I can't see your voice
but I can hear your style
when your electronic kites
land in my box

It takes a while
for me to reply

I've been writing poetry
in the middle of marketing meetings
looking for a way
to position our story

Your tried to take it with you
even when the classics said
that you couldn't

Your handmade journals
were packed by size—
not enough baggage claim
tickets for what you left behind

There was a kiss
that made you feel
like you were set up

It was poetry in a night
where poets need gimmicks
to be heard but all you needed
was enough space
to send the kind of love
that's only practiced
by political prisoners

Or to dream

of holding me tight
inside the eye of a hurricane
with a lyrical name just to
find that all of it was real

FRENCH ROAST

Jet-lagged lovemaking
like dope-dick sex

Hotel Très Nicole
is blessed now

Téléphone ring-ring
and we finger-draw
on windows
fogged with kisses

No central heating for
rain breakfast

La Pigalle positions
put some jelly
on her fresh—

ooooo la la tongue it right
there

My funky mademoiselle
on the Boulevard San-Michel

striking expatriate poses
by the Seine

Nasty French cabrona
works in American-style café

says she don't know English—
in English

TEN-POUND DRAW

On my first trip to London, I learned that the best way to see the city was from the top of a red double-decker bus. If you want to be loved on the first night in more than one position, you have to help with the cooking. On my second trip to London, I learned that the best way to get your smoke on was to first find out where all the Black faces live, so I rode the tube to Brixton Station and found them all over the world living at the end of the line. Came out the station and at the top of the escalator I saw Brotherman selling oils, incense, and sending orders into his cell phone. You think righteousness must be a booming market. The Black girls the Black girls the block girls smile and insist that I am Pakistani when I say that I am Nuyorikistani, so I talk como like this y como like that y como like kikireeboo mandinga, *no doubt, it's all good, I am all of that if you want me to be, but do you know where I can find a ten-pound draw?* No luck finding the Parliament funk, and Roger from Reading said I can't ask for a dime bag, so I buy ten bottles of Egyptian musk and show Brotherman the thirst in my eyes. He leads me to the smoke for a small finder's fee. I am willing to take these chances in spite of the suspicious glances, but just in case, I buy a Big Ben postcard, address it c/o the Crazy Bunch, NYC, and write: "Yo, if I don't make it back home/I was thinking about ya'll/when I went to this place called Brixton/looking for a ten-pound draw."

BLACK BOOTS

Title for a jazz
Riff

A catwalk
Strut

Fifth Avenue
Stroll

Black boot leather
Bass

Fashion honey look
Good as

Hell

STOP SIGNS

I started this poem on the ride back to Heathrow. It could have been the A Train to Harlem, but the stars in the magazine would have said the same thing: Cancer has difficult choices ahead. Virgo finds romance in unlikely places. In the middle of Piccadilly Circus, Eros points the wrong way. Cool-ass swans break off into a ballet of six and suggest that I leave you a note before my flight. They say, *Damn, bro, her Spanish is good, too.* I felt like telling you that I'm not sure how one is supposed to read the signs unless they're falling all over you. If it was up to me, I would grab the ones that shoot across the sky, shake them hard one time, blow on them for good luck, and let them roll. But I had to catch myself before I slipped and broke something, so I flipped it one time: *If you can be with the one you love/don't love the one you're with.* Now I'm laughing through turbulence, replaying the mistake I made in calling you "mami," even after you told me you ain't into that papi thing, you know that ay papi si papi cojelo papi que es tuyo papi thing and I said, Okay, baby, okay sugar, I can call you honey, negra, don't you know you my sweetheart, boo?

SHIT TO WRITE ABOUT

The last time I saw Kriptonite, he had a bottle fight with his girlfriend. He stopped me in front of Gaddafi's and asked me to write something sweet for her. He said it should be something like the poem I wrote for Nestor's girl on Valentine's Day. He asked me to recite that poem. The poem went like this:

The longer I look
for something to say,

the harder I search
for another way

to show you my love

I don't have a rose or
a box of chocolates
to send in place
of my heart

But I can start
with a bouquet
of I love you &
I miss you, close
your eyes, and feel
me kiss you

If I could, I would
turn into Hallmark
and send myself
express

But all I have

is this poem
to show
that I love you more
than I love you less

Krip yelled, "Yeah, yeah, yeah, that's the shit I'm talking about! But, yo, I want mine to be better than that, though. You know what I'm saying?"

"Tell me what you miss about your girl, Krip," I said.

He put his hand on my shoulder, looked into my eyes, and said, "You know how she puts me to sleep? She sings me lullabies while she writes her name in cursive on my back with the tips of her fingernails. She loves it when I run a comb mad soft through her curls. I miss her, yo." He said, like he was lost for the first time.

I remembered the night we were standing in front of 1990 and Krip pointed to a cardboard shrine on the corner, and then he pointed to a row of kicks hanging off the long neck of a light post, the glow-in-the-dark rosaries draped on the rims of yellow candles, eternal flames, untapped forties, unwrapped cigars, tombstones that we visit daily. "Now if you're gonna write about something," Krip said, "that's some shit to write about."

Today his subject was life stories. Unauthorized biographies about players who are reaching the end of their game. "Yo," he started. "I been looking all over for you, man. I heard you was living in Brooklyn now. Coño, you getting fat, kid. God bless you. Word up, bro. Last time I saw you, you looked like you were smoking lovely. Not for nothing, but ninjas were saying that you were down with the dead poets society. Kenny Mac told me you was getting paid to write your life story, and like lately I been having these scrambling nights and hand-to-mouth, baby-crying mornings. I just lost my cousin to the Monster and I'm waiting for a formula that I can drink to grow stronger. The Boys are blowing us off the corners like ghost-town dirt. I feel like I'm running from a cage, crying when no one is looking, like every day is gonna be the last time I see my son, and then I started thinking, bro, if I wanted to write a book, how much you think my life would be worth?"

WORD TO EVERYTHING I LOVE

I feel like dropping some bombs tonight. I have a milk crate bursting at the handles with muses that look like 3 x 7 memo pads, but I only need a minute of your time.

If I told you that your woman was playing you dirty, and you asked if I was for real, I would say, *Word. That's my word to everything I love.* Only because that's what Brother Lo says when he wants you to believe him more than you believe in the god of your choice. These poets who don't even know it will not put their palms on a stack of bibles or swear on the soul of an unborn child. If you find out that they're lying, you can have everything they love.

Here's bomb no. 1: I want to give a shout-out to all those lyric poets who cried behind a low score and left the short circuit through the back door. This is my word to everything I love: When you come back home, you might expect welcome mats of *Damn, where you been? You look good. Is there any-thing I can do for you? Anything you need?* But these are the same mats you stepped on before.

When you come back home, you might expect the spotlight to be as bright as the last time you left the stage, but the page got turned out and you got erased from the next chapter.

When you come back home, your beloveds will ask if you're working your steps and you'll say that you closed your eyes, took one giant step, and never looked back. *Word, to everything I love.*

After you make the love you dream of making, you come home to clean your closets. You keep the phone nearby just in case you bump into half of something that will bring you back and hit you where it hurts.

This blockbuster I give to the word hitters who love to shadowbox back-stage. Let me make a short story shorter. Let me tell you about the night I walked Magda to the supermarket. It snowed so much you could have saved this story in a snow globe. The whole Goya bean section knew we were in love. I carried her ginger, garlic, and twist-off mop in one hand and orange juice and scented candles in another. She gave me her tongue in the vestibule and told me a secret.

The next morning, we met in a garden filled with computers. We download-ed all kinds of flowers and trees. *Word to everything I love.*

Like that, Magda rollerbladed to the clinic with good news. Don't you un-derstand? This is for you repeat offenders in the final round. For those of you who need new material. This is the song of the Almost & the Was. The call you get on a lifeline. Sounds like tears dropping into a voicemail. Imagine the miscarried having its last word. She would have wanted to wear ponytails to class picture day. She would have sketched a poem and left it on my pillow. She was surrounded by a circle of street pigeons in a city square. Today I missed a train stop thinking of what her name would have been.

NOTES FOR A SLOW JAM

The Notes

You want to play this like Petrarch and bless her with a suite of sonnets. But you don't fuck with sonnets, so you decide to write one hundred letters for one hundred days, but you're getting discharged tomorrow morning, so you'll write a slow jam on the back of this patient Bill of Rights.

Yesterday, your roommate asked if you had a love in the world. You told him about the night you watched Laura network a velvet lounge as Wynton Marsalis played a blues tribute for Albert Murray. During a solo, you heard yourself blow a quick *oh shit who is that* riff, but a little voice convinced you that a woman whose laugh could play with music was too good for you.

Your roommate says, "Damn, that's messed up," and went to the dayroom before you could tell him that the first time she said, "Yes," you stayed in bed with her for three days, had breakfast specials delivered, and listened to Robin Harris snap on Bebe's kids. You had her laugh all to yourself.

Right now, you're looking out the window feeling the poem she always wanted about to drop like heavy rain slapping the swing seats in Mount Morris. Time to play diamonds before they call a melancholy snack time. Stray dogs bark at a soundproof window. The bass line sinks and all you want to know is where's your funny valentine.

The Slow Jam

This is the poem you always wanted.

I've turned into a fire-can crooner
to sing you this slow jam,
a farewell greeting no sooner
than the sun set on our meeting,
I had a song for you.

But first
I had to sample
from the midnight "Quiet Storm" like
break to make up,
make up to break up,
and break up to wake up.

I was a three-time loser,
fell in heart over
head—not even a chance
to carve the initials
of our romance
on the bark of a tree.

There's nothing, no one left
to point at and say, *It's all because of you,*
so I have an encounter session
with my bathroom mirror.

Those black crescents under my eyes
tried to cover the cries
that fell on the street as I peaked
on a broken heart binge.

Had to get high so I play
Angel's Social Club where I find
the answer boiling in a jukebox—

pick a song.

Hip-hoppin' through life I thought salsa
was just for the rice & beans—
I was wrong.

You'd probably think I'm high right now
if I told you that Tito Rojas was a Greek playwright
or that Euripides had his own conjunto.

Listen to the tragic hero
chilling on the corner,

epics and shit
spilling from his mouth.

A chorus throws gifts
off a rooftop.

Ay ay ay
Y dicen que los hombres
nunca, nunca deben llorar.

I look into the bathroom mirror
one more time before I chase
you away, and just in case
you don't speak Spanish,
here's some Muddy Waters

Like you can spend what you ain't got
And you can't lose what you never had.

My pockets are empty,
and I'm letting you go without a fight,
but before you go,
here's that poem
you always wanted.

III. THE NEW BOOGALOO

THE NEW BOOGALOO

There's a disco ball
spinning starlight
on the New Boogaloo.

Tell Sonia
that we got bombs
ready to drop,
that our soneros
are ready to sing
to those flowers
that did not survive
Operation Green Thumb.

Tell Dennis
that the renaissance
he's been looking for
is ready to set up shop,
and dreams have decided
to take responsibility
for themselves.

Tell Marcito
that painters are eating pirajuas
sitting on milk crates
and kicking it with poets
who are bored
with keeping it real.

Tell Rosalia
the Reverend Pedro
is on the rooftop
handing out passports
because the spaceship casita
is about to take off.

Que como like
a Brook Avenue Bombaso,
we gonna make you dance.
Que como like un cocotaso limpio,
we gonna make your head rock.

So tell Pachanga
that si no hablas Español—
bienvenido.

That si no hablas Inglés—
bienvenido.

And don't forget
to tell Mikey
that if we have to shoot it up
we gonna shoot it up
mainline,
mainland,
mainstream,
underground
until we catch your vein.

So take this sound
to your grave
and tell the whole block
that a Bambula-building session
is about to begin,
and it's gonna be like
two church boys
talking loud on the train,
praising the Lord
in Spanglish hip-hop speak
like check it:

Pero que son
yo se que fui the Lord, son

eso que mira you know
what it is fam—
we keep the Bible real, kid
tu me entiende
porque he wants me to learn
he told me, sun
to bring my notebook, sun
y mira I was like Whoa
when Reverend Pedro
was waiting for me
with a passport
and he told me
that this time
we gonna die knowing
how beautiful
we really are

POET LOOKING FOR FREE GET HIGH

You just came off a mountain where you used to get high by looking at a hawk spread its wings and take over the sky with a gangster lean. You lost your breath one morning looking at the snowcapped trees turn silver a second before the day broke into something new. But you keep coming back to this poem like roses are red and violets are blue for the lady who rushes out of the building, digging sleep out of her eyes. There used to be a day when her smile could make rain go away and her voice could heal you into a new soul.

"Rose, you still out here?" You check her as she walks by.

"I'm just waiting for this nightmare to end, baby." She stops by a sideview mirror to apply a new coat of cherry-flavored lip gloss. Humming something like *you've forgotten the words "I love you,"* she walks onto Park Avenue and announces a grand opening.

Lately, Magda—my lady—has been crying because she's happy. She used to work under the traffic lights by the train track. When you return from the supermarket, you hand her a loaf of Italian bread for the sandwiches. You tell her that it's time to stop writing about Snow White, Big Leslie, Honey, Rose, and Cinderella. You pour yourself a glass of ginger ale and watch the kids on the playground turn gold through the sparkling soda. A bronze seal sprinkles water on their rhymes.

After breakfast, we fall asleep listening to "Salsa con Polito." You dream of breaking news: Polito Vega interrupts the broadcast to announce that you found a new voice. Magda says, "You can't throw it back in God's face. You can't steal it like you stole sleep from your mother. Now you can get high and it won't cost you anything, Pa." She kisses your third eye and we bless a new love seat. You feel the old poems dying in the *if it ain't rough, it ain't right* sanitation trucks pissing on the street 'round midnight. It's been a long time, you say, since you paid for that dream where you never hit the floor. It cost you more than you can afford to get to the bottom of things without having to pay a fare.

OPEN MIC AT MAKE THE ROAD BY WALKING, INC.

Caminante, no hay camino. Se hace camino al andar.
—Antonio Machado

If it all starts at home, then you're grateful
when your students present you with a cherry
blossom bouquet stolen from a Bronxville garden.

Back in Bushwick, running down a block
stained with family secrets, they finally
discover metaphor: JR says, *I'm glad
to be out of that white-boy air.*

Tonight's open mic starts with an MC battle
on a cinder-block stage.

If you're not careful you can have your heart
snatched from its socket, sprinkled on a tobacco
leaf, rolled up and smoked.

The day-care picture-book readers ring rosies
and duck gooses around plastic pink chairs—
you know you are in the right place where
struggle speaks two languages, where the over-
worked pay membership dues with boleros.

You hope the jokes about dirty sneakers &
generic blue jeans will not lead to a vicious
paper chase, that when roads are finally made,
corner drugstore cowboys will be left without
their cocktail rocks, their quicksilver last words,
that when the analysts visit us with lab reports
that erase the high octave lean of our baseball
caps, the hip-hop of our new sun language,
that we will hijack their studies and write
the next line of poetry by which the world
will choose to live.

CRAZY BUNCH BARBEQUE AT JEFFERSON PARK

This is definitely for the brothers who ain't here,
who would've said I had to write a poem
like a list of names on a memorial
that celebrated our own Old-Timer's Day.

For those of us who age in hood years,
surviving the trade-off was worth writing
our names on the wall and telling the world
that we were here forever.

The barbeque started with a snap session.
Jerry had the best snap of the day when he said
that Skinicky's family was so poor, and the fellas
yelled, *How poor*, and Jerry said so poor
that on Thanksgiving they had to eat
turkey-flavored Skittles.

The laughter needed no help after we exposed
the stretch marks of our growing pains.

Phat Phil had the grill on lock. He slapped
my hand when I tried to cook an extra thigh.

Yo, he said.
Go find something to do.
Write a poem.
Write something.
Do something.
I got this.
I'm the Chef.
You the Poet.
Write about how you glad to be here.
Look at the little boy on the baseball diamond.
Look at him run circles around second base.

Today is his birthday.
Write about how the wind
Is trying to steal his red balloon.

It used to take a few shots of something
strong before we could say, *I love you.*
We have always known how to curse &
bless the dead. Now we let the silence
say it, and like the little boy's sneakers
disappearing in a cloud of dirt, we walk
home in the sun, grown up and full.

This is definitely for the brothers who ain't here,
who would have demanded I write a poem
about how we beat a hood year, and surviving
the trade-off was worth writing our names
on the wall just to let the world know
that we were here forever.

WRITING ABOUT WHAT YOU KNOW

I.

In the story, Papo is on a class trip to the Aguilar branch of the New York Public Library. His name is Papo because seven out of ten brothers in El Barrio, Los Sures, Loisaida, Mott Haven, Humboldt Park, and most of Willimantic, Connecticut, are named Pito, Papo, Chano, Flaco, Piloto, or Waneko. These are names that should make you dream of Taínos in battle with Cristobal and his crew.

Up and down the block there are jingles for manteca, yuca, tamarindo, metadona, plátano maduro, y pan caliente and Papo is trying to listen to the head librarian lecture on the value of the Dewey decimal system. "If you need something on Earth Science, you first go to the card catalog and—." All Papo can hear is the wahwahwahwahwah of a scared police siren speeding toward Paladino.

He turns his head to the Express Book section. There's a book with a picture of his block on the cover. He can tell by the identification tags on the walls. They tell him who loved who and for how long. The book says that there is poetry inside. The title buzzes on Papo's tongue like a biscuit of neon. The poet is standing under a light post. Puerto Rican flags dangle chest first from fire escapes. A cipher of late-night tree blazers share a large cup of sesame juice at the cuchifrito stand.

II.

Papo tells his creative writing teacher that he's having a hard time finding something to write about. The teacher says, "Write about what you know. And remember—don't tell me, show me."

That night Papo was chilling in front of Gaddafi's with Baby Face Nelson and Green Eye Raymond. A sea-blue BMW drives by with a jukebox in the trunk. The Yellow-Top Crew just cracked their first bottle of champagne. The tempo for Papo's first writing assignment is set by a round of automatic shots ringing from the rooftops. The shots are followed by a heavy, deep, hip-hop jeep bassline-thump and a fury of congas warning you to strap in and hold on tight.

GREEN EYE RAYMOND   Sounds like they pullin' somebody's wig back. How many shots you heard?

PAPO   Like ten.

BABY FACE NELSON   Word. That's what I heard. And those shots sounded like they had names and addresses.

III.

Later, the streets go back to what they were saying, and Papo looks out the window and writes his assignment:

TO LIVE AND DIE IN SPANISH HARLEM

His name was Papo.
We didn't know his real name.

He lived and died in Spanish Harlem.

IV.

Before Papo begins teaching his workshop at Phoenix House, he is asked to give a self-disclosure. "The Hawk was out the night my life changed," he starts. "He was rocking icicle-shaped sideburns and had a wicked wind chill on his back. I walked out of my building and Doña Pancha was pushing her shopping cart up the handicap ramp. She blessed me and told me to be careful because Lexington was hot. A grapevine warning went out to all the Scramblers. Chuck Norris and his partner Chewbaca were in the blue Taurus that night. My eyes were glazed with a first-bag note. I felt silky. Everything made warm sense. I saw a badge tinkle in a factory window. I thought it was a sparkler. 'Yo,' a customer says, 'the Boys are gonna jump.' Before I realized that I made a direct sale, four car doors slammed, one right after the other, like a clave short of a beat. Black glocks pointed deadly aim and promised salvation if I stood frozen. It was the sound of the uptown blue man group delivering a one-way ticket to Central Booking. The package included unlimited time-shares and revolving door insurance policies. The city insulated my stomach with inch-thick slices of baloney and American cheese. Now, I'm here to tell you: I've slept through seven-hour trips to Paris. I've been on long, hot, yellow school-bus rides with unruly preschoolers yelling all the way to Jones Beach. And I've been on a cruise-controlled ride in an amethyst-colored Benz from London to Brighton, *Kind of Blue* on the tape deck and a countryside vista to dream with. But the longest ride I've ever been on was in the back of an NYPD caged bus, hands cuffed in front of me, counting the seconds it took to cross the long, white-sand bridge that separates Rikers Island from the rest of the world. I remembered hanging out in a lobby and a bunch of us were collecting change for a sponge ball and Rudy was talking about going to jail like a college-bound senior anticipating his first day of class. *When I go to jail . . .* I called my mother with my first click. She cried and told me she would run to the end of the world for me. I sold a pack of flavors for a six-minute click, a sheet of paper, a pencil, and a stamped envelope. I wrote Nef. I told her that I missed the way orange-blossom lotion moistens in her belly button and the way she could compress love into seventeen syllables. I told her that black & white photographs make rock bottoms look sweet. I promised that I would stop feeding the wind that takes all the lives in the urban studies and that from now on I would use true colors to write about what I know."

KICKING

Skipping rocks on a Lisbon Falls lake, my cousin Vic tells me that I need to stop wishing for a magic potion. "But peep this for a taste," he says. "On the one hand, you're down with the Seven Dwarves whereby you owe you owe you owe you owe you owe. The Boys are hunting you down and you couldn't buy the tombstone your mother picked because her insurance money turned into a meteor where your pockets used to be. On the other hand, though," he continues, "picture yourself waiting for your son to come out of school so you could go skip rocks. When you stop at the house you find out that you're going to have another child and this time your wife thinks it's a boy because the cowlick at the top of your son's head is curling clockwise. Your son asks you why you like skipping rocks so much and you say because one day you made a flat stone skip almost ten times while your cousin drew a picture of your life with his hands."

UN AMOR DE LA CALLE

Last Friday night you was walking down Lexington Avenue when Truth called you from across the street and said he had something to say. Before you reached the corner he said, "Whaddup, my nigga? Ain't seen you in a while. Act like you don't know nobody." You tell him that you been working on some fiction. Truth said, "That don't mean you can't call a brother, send him a note or something." Lies came out of the bodega, walking sideways. He put a box of strawberry blunt wraps in his pocket, gave me a weak power grip and said the jump-off was ready. Deceit was chilling by the corner telling Duplicity that if his wife comes around, tell her that he got arrested and that he'll be in Central Booking for the weekend. Fidelity was doing pull-ups on a tenement scaffold. Sincerity stuck her head out the window and told him to come up, dinner was ready. Dishonesty pulled up in a black beamer with South Carolina plates. He was recruiting for a drive-by on some old beef. Reason called from across the street and reminded you to buy tickets for the church bus ride to Atlantic City on Sunday. Connivance was standing behind a dumpster, stacking bricks into an empty DVD box. Honesty waved from the back of a southbound M101, said you should use her number. Spit was falling from the corner of Scheme's mouth as he devised a plan to make lots and lots of ducats, and that's when Collusion pulled up and said, "If, of course, you still doing that kind of thing."

LOOK WHAT I FOUND

Two brothers rap
in front of St. Paul's.

Brother One
boasts of his platonic relationship with Jesus,
Sunday miracles, and baptized dreams.

He said, *I pray.*
I pray every day
and I pray every night.

Brother Two egged him on with a
Speak & Say That.

Then Brother One said,

You hear me?
I pray every night.

And then he lowered
his voice to a hymn
and said,

Even when
I'm high.

REFLECTIONS ON THE METRO-NORTH, SPRING 1997

Monday morning and you're on the 11:12 a.m. from Poughkeepsie to
  Grand Central.

You're on your way to let the judge know that you went to go tell it on a
  mountain.

The sun is following this updated reflection.

Doors close and the train whispers to you gospel-humming *I'm starting all
  over again.*

Like the seagulls skipping on the Hudson,
you know where the wind is guiding you these days.

Your jukebox love-song girl used to sleep on your shoulder as you
watched ducks dance in the street, wishing you could start over.

Sing Sing walls rap in electrocuted time & handcuffed verses.

Corporate Card has an office sitting on his lap.

Your stomach does a somersault when the train steams into the Bronx.
(Grab your mental mops from your soul bucket and clean this land of
smoke shops, death in hip-hops, Black justice in the guns of white cops.)

You heard Mickey Mouse is about to open shop on 7th Avenue.

Oh shit, you see that? TNT is eight deep. Don't sleep. To be aware is to be
  alive.

The train rumbles by the bodega where once a crew of cold turkeys
attacked your panic buttons and told you to pawn your passport.

From corner to corner moves your old fortune teller.

Mami Cuca and Miss Mary compose state-of-the-block speeches on the stoop.

Next stop: times are square for real and curbs have PG ratings.

Make sure you take your personal belongings and leave the past where it belongs.

Remember to tell the judge that your ghost was arrested this morning.

Don't forget what Brother Lo said one night: "Religion is for people who are afraid to go to hell; spirituality is for people who been there."

Bopping back into this strange fruit, you take out a prayer, puff on some peace, and put some in the stash for later.

SOME "AFTER WORDS"

In the spring term of my senior year of high school—1985—I did my first poetry reading with my primary mentor, Ed Randolph. I say "did" my reading because I come from the school of poets who go "do" readings instead of performances. Readings, in those days, were connected to what you wrote on paper and delivered from a manuscript. The poem on the page was your score, so the poem on the stage became your jam session. Performances, on the other hand, veered into the murk of persona, spotlight, and gimmick. After the reading, Ed told me that I should never explain a poem away before reading it to an audience. *Let the poem do the work,* he said.

By the time I arrived at the Nuyorican Poets Café in the fall of 1991, my apprenticeship with Ed had served me well. I was spared the wrath and humiliation of the late Steve Cannon, founder of A Gathering of the Tribes, who, from the back of the bar, would demand that you "Read the goddamn poem!" if you decided to proffer a lengthy preamble before you spit. In his view, not only were you copping a plea, but you were cutting into the next poet's minutes on the open mic. My first night at the Nuyorican, I stepped to the mic and said, "This poem is called _____," and ripped it. Sometimes, after that first night, I didn't even bother sharing the title—I just went right into the first line of a poem, which would have an immediate silencing effect on an audience. These are lessons that you don't learn as a first-year MFA student. You learn them from what Etheridge Knight called "poeting."

Similar to copping a plea before reading a poem, reissuing a book or providing a preface can come across as a botched rescue mission. After reading Adrienne Rich's essay "When We Dead Awaken: Writing as Re-Vision,"

I was emboldened by the act of revision—as it was framed by Rich—to be more an exercise in revisitation than a matter of fixing a comma or two. Revisiting *Smoking Lovely* was akin to returning to the old neighborhood, but this time I was clean, rehabilitated, focused, employed, productive, married, a father, and a teacher, and I also learned that the bodega where I found openings and endings to my poems was no longer there. You see faces, but you forget names. Not only has the block changed, but you have undergone some alterations as well.

*

Smoking Lovely was my Program book. In the Program, I learned how to tell on myself, how to roll up my socks and boxer briefs so tight that I could bounce them off a wall. I learned how to play an encounter group and be confronted on my negative attitude. I washed cooking vats so deep that you could climb into them and kneel—hide, if need be—and being the sucker-for-love-ass negus that I am, I almost fell in love in the Program.

The one thing I didn't do in the Program was write. I scratched, cried, scribbled, doodled, wondered, and dreamt, but I didn't write.

The Counselors in the Program used to say that if you have one foot in the future and one foot in the past, chances are that you might be pissing all over the present. Tooled with the Counselors' zazen-type advice, once I left the Program, I rarely talked about my dragon-chasing days, the trips to Central Booking, or my time in the Program. My rock bottom was a goose-feather pillow compared to my Day Ones' splintered park-bench testimonials, so I kept my war stories to myself. Randomly, however, flashbacks and demons started joining me for my morning Bustelo or a subway ride to work. They forced me to relive and examine what I like to call my "bop through the dark wood." Books do that. They creep up on you from behind, cover your eyes with their hands, and yell, "Guess who?"

*

I write books. I don't write poems. I think it was Jack Spicer who said that. It's hard to pull a poem from one of my working manuscripts for submission to a literary journal without including the body from which it was extract-ed. In a letter dated February 20, 1993, my second mentor, Raymond R. Patterson, after seeing me do a reading at St. Mark's Church, wrote, "I think you are writing one poem. I don't mean the same poem over and over again. I mean that all of your poems seem to be part of one large poem, and it makes me think of an epic—a tale of the tribe—as someone once called it." According to Miguel Algarín, founder of the Nuyorican Poets Café, in the outlaw tradition of Nuyorican Poetry, the poet is a troubadour telling the story of the street to the street. Except this time, with *Smoking Lovely*, I wasn't quite sure who I was telling a story to; it felt like I was in the Program dumping my shit on anyone who was willing to listen.

On the day that the first edition of this book was officially published in 2003, I had to wait at a Lower East Side storage facility for a Yellow Truck to deliver fifteen hundred copies. My publisher had an important meeting at his day job at Citibank, where he was an IT guy. Gone were the days of meeting my editor at Café Un Deux Trois for lunch and receiving my author copies at my agent's office. My editor at Norton, Jill Bialosky, had rejected *Smoking Lovely*. The book just wasn't ready. The rejection, years later, felt valid. I don't believe in jinxes, but having been an assistant to the legendary literary agent Marie Brown, and a rights manager at Henry Holt, I had rocked in the publishing world long enough to know that a writer's second book sets the tone for their body of work; it sends a signal that they're in this for the long haul.

I'm a book lover, so fonts and spines and jacket covers and title pages have to be correct. If you know book lovers, they have a tactile relationship with their books. We sort by alphabet, genre, school, or publisher. We call our libraries "stacks," and we are hard-pressed to lend a book without an imme-diate reminder to return when done. Ask a book lover where they feel most safe, and more than likely they'll say a bookstore or a library. When I pulled the first copy out of a box, I had a gigantic shaking-my-head moment before texting SMH was a thing. I had to collect call all the tools of gratitude and humility that I learned in the Program. Shit, I said, be happy, you wrote another book. Not necessarily a better book, but another book to add to my oeuvre. My ego had to be checked that afternoon, and I realized that my ego had mutated in the spotlight of what poet Major Jackson calls a "celebrity poet." I was expecting the book to clap back at me, but the only sound I remember was the beeping Yellow Truck backing out of the loading dock.

I have been asked many times, "What's wrong with the book? Why don't you like it?" Alright, then, let's start with the original cover: dope imagery, for sure, especially the use of De La Vega's East Harlem wall-length ode to Picasso's *Guernica*, but I wasn't crazy about the design, the busyness of the cover, and its attempt at providing translatable images. Since that day, I have been adamant about my books having clean lines that don't obstruct your sight nor literalize the content. Next: the jacket copy. Writing your own copy is not a good idea. You start making claims on a book that you might not be able to substantiate. I rather a publisher take a stab at the copy to see if they *get* the book. Otherwise, if I write my own copy, I end up doing stupid shit like comparing Lexington Avenue in East Harlem to Yoknapatawpha. At the very least, my heart was definitely in conflict with itself. Lexington was more an Afro-Boricua Macondo, and it's true, my work has always been entrenched in a sense of place, but I was no Faulkner, didn't want to be Faulkner; shit, I had never read Faulkner. But when the book fell off the truck, I was suddenly on Front Street being jacked by my own sense of pretension and fraudulence. Was I a writer for real? Or was I pretending to be one? I didn't have to look at the book for very long before I stacked the boxes—one of which was ripped open at a corner—locked up the storage unit, and drove home with a single copy in my backpack. I didn't even want to *give* the book away.

But the real issue was that some of the poems in the book were wack. Constantly being in front of a live audience, along with smoking woos and sniffing bundles of "9½" or "Knockout" had dulled my discipline, stunted my love of reading, and impeded my practice. Every standing ovation, every offer of sex and drugs, every video shoot, every VIP section, had tricked me into thinking that my work was good, and I started writing for the "audience." But it wasn't all bad. I learned how to improvise and edit on the spot, and I had a good run on the circuit. Made a few racks and even earned some frequent flyer miles. My poems became my ultimate passport. I traveled from Miami to San Francisco, from Harlem to Haarlem. But by the time *Smoking Lovely* was published, it was clear that some of the poems were really prose broken into lines that were trapped in lazy, unimaginative, clichéd street tropes, which is typically the case when a writer thinks that the raw experience of their life would make for a good book.

If, as Mary Oliver claimed in *A Poetry Handbook,* a poem is like a house and each stanza is like a room in that house, then I wanted to bring a demolition crew to *Smoking Lovely.* Especially after the second edition (2005), to which I added a few more poems in a section called "Residue" and changed the cover image to a single detail from De La Vega's mural: a ghostly white figure in blackface—in blackface—smoking a cigarette. *My man,* I needed someone to say, *what the fuck are you doing?*

*

My misgivings about the book were common knowledge in the poetry/ spoken word scene. When Steve Sapp, cofounder of Universes, Inc., approached me about adapting *Smoking Lovely* for the stage, I texted him back and said, "I think *Smoking Lovely* is best left alone, bro." We didn't speak for years after that. Shortly thereafter, at a party for Tato Laviera at El Maestro in the Bronx, poet and NYU professor Urayoán Noel asked me if I would be open to talking about *Smoking Lovely* for his dissertation. I told Urayoán, "Broquí, the less said about *Smoking Lovely,* the better." If you mentioned the book to me during that time in my writing life, it was as if we were in an episode of Abbott and Costello and you were the person asking for directions to the Susquehanna Hat Company, and I was the dude punching a hole through a boater hat.

Two books later, I learned that 1) Raymond Patterson was right: I am writing one large poem and 2) part of my practice is taking a risk and forgetting who my readers are until I hear from them. I started to meet poets like Dr. Randall Horton, a fully tenured professor who did Fed time, smuggled bricks internationally, and after reading *Smoking Lovely* said, "Mane, I know you know, Willie." Or Jon Sands, who, upon arrival in New York City, started his teaching career facilitating creative writing workshops in an East Harlem needle exchange program and used my book as required reading. It wasn't until I went to visit the exchange as a guest poet that I understood the book's resonance. I started to meet people from Harlem who were upset at the cosmetic and gentrified changes in Harlem and had thanked me for the poems. Shortly before I agreed to reissue *Smoking Lovely,* I received an email with a link to an interview with poet Danez Smith, which was published in the *Guardian*. Danez was asked for the title of a book that changed their life and Danez replied, "In my freshman year of college I was given a copy of *Smoking Lovely* by Willie Perdomo, and it was the first time I had seen a book of poetry. Perdomo's poems helped me make sense of the addiction that lived in my family and me, while also showing me how alive poems could be on the page."[1] Writers love these kinds of reminders. They're like a tap on the shoulder when you're looking the wrong way. I wrote the book for the same reason it impacted Danez: to make sense of my life, to make sense of the changes and chaos in my neighborhood, to bring the stage to the page. But the most lasting and significant moment connected to the book's publication was a phone call I received about a week after the book was published. (I forgot about this moment while I was busy hating on the book. This was a landline call, by the way.) That evening, my wife answered the phone. The call was for me. I asked her who was on the line and she said she didn't know. I took the receiver, said, "Hello," and a late-night DJ baritone voice responded, "Hey, Willie, it's Gil Scott." He went on to say some kind words about the book, but I was stuck after he mentioned his name. I only remember hanging up and saying to my wife, "Oh shit, that was Gil Scott-Heron." Said his full name just like that. Earlier that year, I had sent Gil Scott my book to request a blurb, but he never got back to me, so I forgot about it. I don't remember how I found his address, but the book landed in his hands, and what added to the call's importance was the memory it triggered. Seven years before that phone call, I was in the Program, and one Sunday, after an approved weekend visit, Lou, one of my roommates, returned with a copy of *Vibe* magazine that was earmarked to the "20 Questions" section. Lou said, "This you, bro?" He pointed to a question that read, "Why do we think Willie Perdomo is going to be the next Gil Scott-Heron?" The answer to that question is really an exploration of how poets get to the Other Side, but what you should know is that Gil Scott taught me how to use poetry as a mode of definition, and awareness as the ultimate weapon in Citizenry.

*

---

1 Danez Smith, "Books that Made Me," *Guardian*, October 20, 2018. https://www. theguardian.com/books/2018/oct/20/books-that-made-me-danez-smith.

That fall, after the book was published, I received an email from my publisher asking me to meet at the main branch of the Brooklyn Public Library at Grand Army Plaza. *Smoking Lovely* had just won the 2004 PEN Beyond Margins Award. As of 2020, this particular PEN award has also undergone dramatic revision—the award is now called the PEN Open Book Award and comes with a healthy check. When it was named Beyond Margins, it came with zero dollars and was stigmatized as a POC award, but that was okay because I lived a few blocks away from the library, so I walked to get my prize, and, as a total bonus, the great Maestra—novelist Elizabeth Nunez—a champion of Black Carib literature—presented me with the award. The diaspora was giving *and* receiving that day. And, it should be added (something else I lost sight of while I was shitting on the book), that while Norton sent me to do only one reading in DC for my first book, *Where a Nickel Costs a Dime*, and where I stayed in a quaint suite at the Canterbury Hotel and had coffee at the Chaucer Café, *Rattapallax* sent me to Ghana and Chile. So much for the futility of comparing and contrast: my second book went global.

*

Every book has a shelf life. Or, better put, an Amazonian life. Up until this reissue, *Smoking Lovely* was out of print. At one point, signed copies of first editions were going for almost $100 on Amazon. That's Hibiki money. This remix is the third (and final) try. Revising *Smoking Lovely* was like upholstering a favorite love seat, and on some days, it was like replacing a broken refrigerator handle. When I told one of my poet homies that Haymarket Books wanted to reissue the book she said, "You might as well give them a new book. They can get the old book at the library." Audre Lorde is said to have revised up to the last minute of publishing her collected poems; that's three hundred poems that were being seen anew up to the moment of death. So, in this makeover, you will find a rededication, Urayoán Noel's introduction, a brief foray into dramatic writing with one of my favorite forms, the 10-minute play, de-italicized Spanish words, and this afterword. As it goes for the Poet, so it goes for the Reader: the book had to be a new experience.

The choices I made to rehaul *Smoking Lovely* were intentional. Along with reconfiguring some pieces into prose poems, I also changed the POV in some pieces, switching from "I" to "You." The "I" can be dangerous. With the "I," you can fall into traps of self-mythologized, self-exoticized, quasi-confessional poems devoid of funk. The "You," though, is very much like a Nod. The "You" speaks to you even when you ain't trying to listen. The "You" is the Reader, too. The "You" is there to say, "You're gonna be okay, bro," or, "You ain't shit, bro. How you gonna sell your mother's graduation ring?"

*

One last thing about revision: salsa music is my uptown, north of 96th Street, after midnight, rum-in-plastic-cups-hangout music. Hip-hop is my booming system and freestyle cipher. Andre Watts playing Liszt is my Sunday sweep-the-rug music as is Aretha Franklin's *Amazing Grace* or Celina Y Reutolio's *Santa Barbara*. But jazz? Jazz is where I find the changes and alternate takes. Jazz is where I discover my aesthetics. One night, close to meeting my Haymarket deadline, I was working on this essay and listening to the deluxe edition of *Charlie Parker with Strings*. This is post-Camarillo State Mental Hospital Bird—a lush, romantic, unrequited, orchestrated experiment with second and third takes of "Just Friends" or "April in Paris," and during one retake I remember smiling and feeling like my revisitation process was affirmed. I remember thinking that's how revision works: even Bird didn't get it right on the first try, no matter how high he was flying.

WILLIE PERDOMO
Exeter, New Hampshire
September 14, 2020

ACKNOWLEDGMENTS

Big up to Haymarket Books and the Breakbeat Poet Series for inviting *Smoking Lovely* to the jam.

Nisha Bolsey for your heroic patience.

Maya Marshall for your exactness and compassion.

José Olivarez and Felicia Rose Chavez for *LatiNext*.

Big up to Chicago. One brother said it best, "People sleep on Chicago. Chicago is jukin'."

Jon Sands for swearing by this book and never letting me forget.

Urayoán Noel for your diasporic lens.

Ram Devineni for publishing the original *Smoking Lovely*, twice.

Edwin Torres for chipping in.

To the Stairwell Crew: I guess ya'll could call this a lost brick that I had to re-up on.

RIP, Miguel Algarín.

RIP, Adál Maldonado.

Peace.

ABOUT THE AUTHOR

Photo by Sandra Perdomo

Willie Perdomo is the author of *The Crazy Bunch* (2019), *The Essential Hits of Shorty Bon Bon* (2014), *Smoking Lovely* (2003), and *Where a Nickel Costs of Dime* (1996). Winner of the Foundation for Contemporary Arts Cy Twombly Award for Poetry, the New York City Book Award for Poetry, and the PEN Open Book Award, Perdomo was also a finalist for the National Book Critics Circle Award and the Poetry Society of America Norma Farber First Book Award. He is coeditor of the *Breakbeat Poets Volume 4: LatiNext*. His work has appeared in *New York Times Magazine*, *POETRY*, *Best American Poetry 2019*, and *African Voices*. He is currently a Lucas Arts Literary Fellow, a core faculty member at VONA/Voices of our Nation Writing Workshop, and he teaches English at Phillips Exeter Academy.